TITANOBOA

A First Look

HANNAH GRAMSON

Lerner Publications ◆ Minneapolis

Educator Toolbox

Reading books is a great way for kids to express what they're interested in. Before reading this title, ask the reader these questions:

> What do you think this book is about? Look at the cover for clues.
>
> What do you already know about Titanoboas?
>
> What do you want to learn about Titanoboas?

Let's Read Together

Encourage the reader to use the pictures to understand the text.

Point out when the reader successfully sounds out a word.

Praise the reader for recognizing sight words such as *had* and *in*.

TABLE OF CONTENTS

Titanoboa 4

You Connect! 21
STEM Snapshot 22
Photo Glossary 23
Learn More 23
Index 24

Titanoboa

Titanoboas were snakes. They lived about fifty-eight million years ago.

They were the biggest snakes ever.

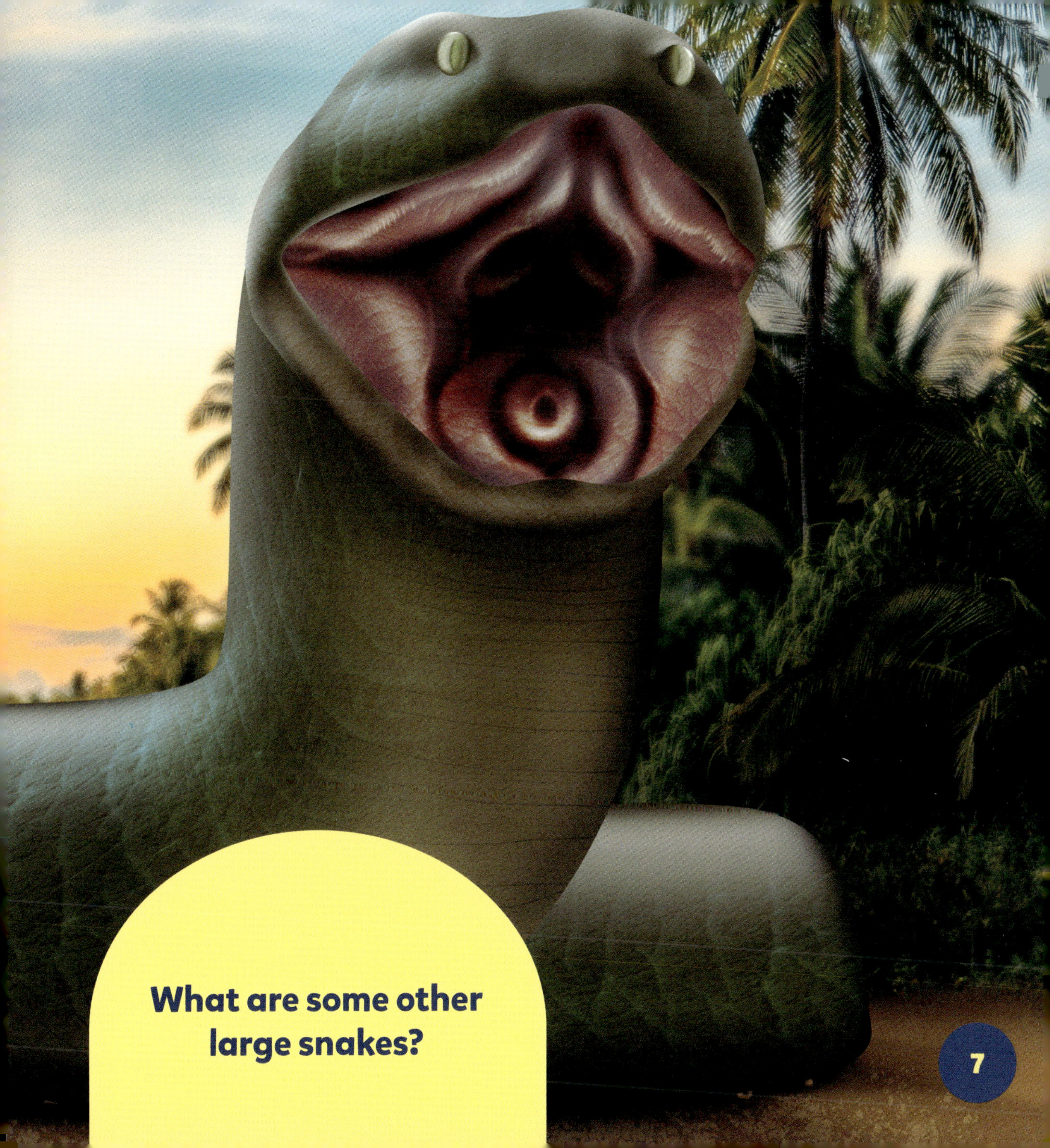

What are some other large snakes?

They were about 50 feet (15 m) long. That's as wide as a basketball court!

They had scales. They had two big fangs.

How were Titanoboas like other snakes?

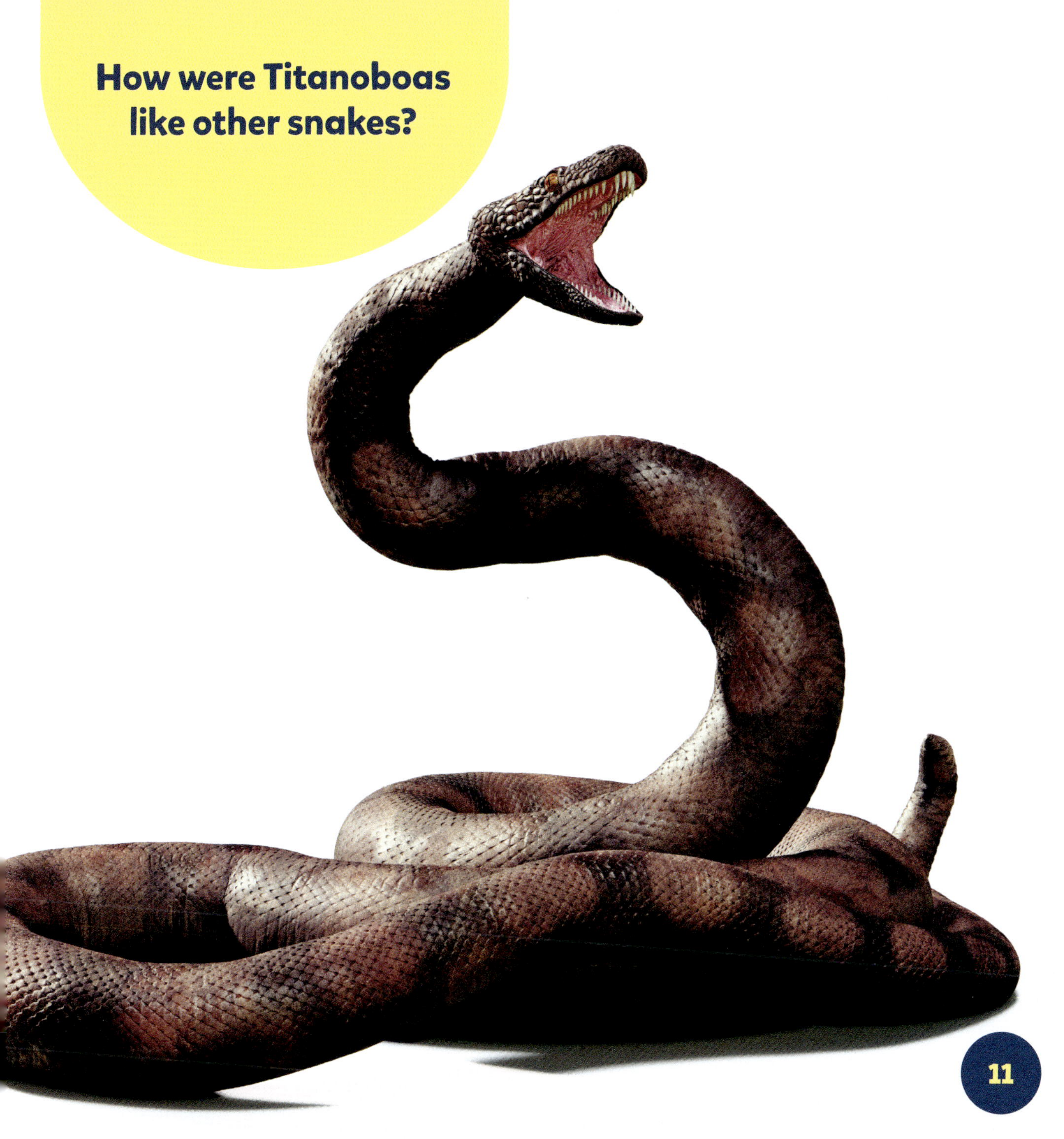

Titanoboas ate large fish and turtles.

They even ate crocodiles.

Their meals were big. They only ate a few times a year.

Titanoboas lived in hot places such as swamps and jungles.

They spent a lot of time in water.

Why do you think they were often in water?

People learned about them
by looking at their bones.

You Connect!

What do you like about Titanoboas?

Would you want to meet a Titanoboa?

What are some other snakes you know about?

STEM Snapshot

Encourage students to think and ask questions as scientists. Ask the reader:

What is something you learned about Titanoboas?

What is something you noticed about the way Titanoboas looked?

What is something you still want to learn about Titanoboas?

Photo Glossary

Learn More

Fowler, Leona. *Snakes*. Enslow, 2024.

Gramson, Hannah. *Tully Monster: A First Look*. Lerner Publications, 2026.

Riggs, Kate. *Snakes*. Creative Education and Creative Paperbacks, 2025.

Index

bone, 20

fang, 10

scale, 10

snake, 4, 6–7, 11

swamp, 16

Photo Acknowledgments

Image credits: MR1805/Getty Images, pp. 5, 8, 12, 19; chingting huang/Getty Images, p. 6; Adisha Pramod/Alamy, p. 7; Dotted Yeti/Shutterstock, p. 11; JA CHIRINOS/Science Source, p. 13; dotted zebra/Alamy, p. 14; Peter Unger/Getty Images, p. 17; Millard H. Sharp/Science Source, p. 20; Kryssia Campos/Getty Images, p. 23. Cover: dotted zebra/Alamy.

Copyright © 2026 by Lerner Publishing Group, Inc.

All rights reserved. International copyright secured. No part of this book may be reproduced, stored in a retrieval system, or transmitted in any form or by any means—electronic, mechanical, photocopying, recording, or otherwise—without the prior written permission of Lerner Publishing Group, Inc., except for the inclusion of brief quotations in an acknowledged review.

Lerner Publications Company
An imprint of Lerner Publishing Group, Inc.
241 First Avenue North
Minneapolis, MN 55401 USA

For reading levels and more information, look up this title at www.lernerbooks.com.

Main body text set in Mikado Medium.
Typeface provided by Hannes von Doehren.

Editor: Nicole Berglund **Photo Editor:** Nicole Berglund

Library of Congress Cataloging-in-Publication Data

Names: Gramson, Hannah, author.
Title: Titanoboa : a first look / Hannah Gramson.
Description: Minneapolis : Lerner Publications, [2025] | Series: Read about prehistoric beasts (read for a better world) | Includes bibliographical references and index. | Audience: Ages 5–8 | Audience: Grades K–1 | Summary: "The Titanoboa was a giant snake that lived many years ago. Discover how this reptile lived, from its habitat to its diet"– Provided by publisher.
Identifiers: LCCN 2024051414 (print) | LCCN 2024051415 (ebook) | ISBN 9798765669082 (lib. bdg.) | ISBN 9798765684726 (pbk.) | ISBN 9798765680490 (epub)
Subjects: LCSH: Titanoboa—Juvenile literature.
Classification: LCC QL666.O63 G7295 2025 (print) | LCC QL666.O63 (ebook) | DDC 597.96/7—dc23/eng/20250318

LC record available at https://lccn.loc.gov/2024051414
LC ebook record available at https://lccn.loc.gov/2024051415

Manufactured in the United States of America
1-1011835-53879-2/19/2025